W9-AOB-618

The Island of Lost Luggage

Native Writers' Circle of the Americas/Wordcraft Circle

First Book Awards

Evelina Zuni Lucero, *Night Sky, Morning Star*

Janet McAdams, *The Island of Lost Luggage*

Series Editor, Geary Hobson

The Island of Lost Luggage

JANET MCADAMS

The University of Arizona Press

Tucson

The University of Arizona Press
© 2000 Janet McAdams
All Rights Reserved

⊗ This book is printed on acid-free, archival-quality paper
Manufactured in the United States of America
First printing

Library of Congress Cataloging-in-Publication Data
McAdams, Janet
The island of lost luggage / Janet McAdams.
    p. cm. — (First book awards)
ISBN 0-8165-2056-9 (pbk.: alk. paper)
1. Central America—Poetry. 2. Nature—Effect of human beings
on—Poetry. I. Title. II. Series.
PS3563.C263   185   2000
813'.6—dc21   99-050807

British Cataloguing-in-Publication Data
A catalogue record for this book is available from the British Library.

Excerpt from "Seascape," from *Sea Change: Poems* by Christopher Howell, L'Epervier
Press, 1985. Reprinted by permission of the author.
Excerpt from "The Moon and the Yew Tree," from *The Collected Poems of Sylvia
Plath,* edited by Ted Hughes. © 1963 by the Estate of Sylvia Plath. Copyright
renewed. Reprinted by permission of HarperCollins Publishers.
Excerpt from "Starring America," from *An Eagle Nation* by Carter Revard. © 1993
Carter C. Revard. Reprinted by permission of The University of Arizona Press.
Excerpt from "The Sonnets to Orpheus," from *The Selected Poetry of Rainer Maria
Rilke,* edited and translated by Stephen Mitchell. Copyright © 1982 by Stephen
Mitchell. Reprinted by permission of Random House, Inc.
Excerpt from "At This Moment of Time," from *Selected Poems: Summer Knowledge*
by Delmore Schwartz, © 1967. Reprinted by permission of New Directions Pub.
Corp.

Publication of this book was made possible in part by a grant from the National
Endowment for the Arts.

FOR MY GRANDMOTHER, WILLIE ELLIS WREN,
AND IN MEMORY OF
MY GRANDMOTHER, CORA MCADAMS MARTIN.

. . . Rescue is only wind at play
on the long prairies of water.
Your choice is to believe it and drown,
or to drown, simply.

—CHRISTOPHER HOWELL

Disturb me, compel me. It is not true
That "no man is happy," but that is not
The sense which guides you. If we are
Unfinished (we are, unless hope is a bad dream),
You are exact. You tug my sleeve
Before I speak, with a shadow's friendship,
And I remember that we who move
Are moved by clouds that darken midnight.

—DELMORE SCHWARTZ

Contents

I

Boulevard of Heroes

I think it's the NEW WORLD rising
like midnight dawn, and it shines
only for safety. . . .
—CARTER REVARD

The Basilica of Our Lady of Good Health
A Postcard

They shaped you from Tzintzingue paste, rich yellow corn
ground with orchid honey. Your gown's stiff hem
would taste sweet against the tongue, the lips

of the pilgrim's kiss I long to give you.
From his shallow cubbyhole, Saint Lucas and his thick cow
are startled by bells that ring for evensong, *Dong, Dong.*

A child with chubby legs sings along; his mother flogs
cheap rosaries, gold-framed portraits of Mexico's brown-faced virgin.
Twice a year you hear our prayers. No, not mine,

but those of pilgrims who crawl across the Plaza Grande,
past the ash tree where Bocanegra defied the Spanish. I lean over
the wrought-iron fence circling the ash and fit my fingers into

five bullet holes. The pilgrims wear white cloaks to hide
their bloody knees. They beg a cure for warts, fits of coughing,
joints so stiff these heartless winter mornings.

Their prayers are dull silver: *milagros* shaped like hands,
like hearts, a horse, a dove, a boy's head turned in profile.
Lady, lean down, I will whisper my questions:

What if my heart grew scales and swam like a fish through my body?
Are there breaking points in the continent of my body?
Is the broken skin of the ash any woman's story?

I place the fish *milagro* inside the deepest bullet hole,
the one shaped like a heart. Listen:
I want a miracle for every part of my body.

El Salvador del Mundo

It's full moon here. Saturn and Jupiter
line up across the tropical sky and we wait,
we wait. Our eyes focus and the sky
becomes a color after all.

It is April, and you are the friend I most long for.
My students line up in their sad rows of chairs
and no longer move me, our little country of unhappiness
exploding over and over. Last night I trailed
a bottle of Tick Tack down Paseo Escalón,
the red label fluorescent in the bright dark
of our altitude.

What is the savior of the world doing
among these wire fences, in all this broken glass?
If the street were a sky, glass would glitter
like stars, a thousand broken pieces along the curb.
The planets would swing on their startled orbits,
the earth, a heavy fist of heart, turn blue as death,
flexing its chambers of love and sorrow,
easing its way into the stone hand of God.

Boulevard of Heroes
San Salvador

The day you took me up there, they marched
in thousands, the red blur tumbling downhill
and Duarte's group, a collection
of white visors—a lie, you said
and you should know. The hot odor
of jacaranda spilled from a tree
where reporters whose names we knew
flashed their cameras and called out
questions to their translators.
I was thirsty. Orange Popsicle
ran down my chin onto my white shirt.
We had our little gringo argument,
hot with politics, full of ourselves.

The students were turning cars over downtown
and they told us to stay in,
boil water, and keep a flashlight handy.
When the theater blew up, I wasn't frightened.
Through the rush of black smoke,
I went back for my camera. I still have
a piece of chrome from the car that exploded.
After the lights failed, a friend took me out
for pizza, and we ate by the yellow glow of a lantern.
I was glad I didn't have to grade papers.
I didn't care if the war went on forever.

Six young men knot kerchiefs over their faces
and hoist the coffin onto their shoulders,
kicking up small clouds of dust
down the Boulevard of Heroes,
across the television screen above the bar.
I could almost imagine the returning army,

home from Honduras. The North Americans wink
and say, "You know, the Football War."
Nothing, after all, in a country where people
die like crazy. That night at the Brit Club,
when you pointed out the women you'd slept with,
I could smell the gin on your breath. Friend, you're
fooling yourself. This is the safest life I know.

The Hands of the Taino

Laid out on vellum, the past
is a long wound. It unfolds
five centuries later,
beneath the heavy pens of scholars.
The world shifts and spins
as the Admiral's bronze astrolabe
measures the paths between stars.
The sky is written in the sea's
uneasy mirror, and mermaids
comb their hair in the distance.
They are not, he writes, *so beautiful
as I have heard.* He dreams of his own
circuitous route to the Heavens.
God and the Crown. Both want too much.

II. GOVERNOR
At Guanahani, they swam to the caravel
bearing parrots and balls of cotton thread,
these people so unlike him they could not
not be saved.
        Too angry to sleep,
the Governor haunts every room in his castle.
The servants whisper in their own tongue.

The severed hands of the Taino
wave in clear salt water,
in pink-tinted water.
They wave as the gold mines dry up,
as the Governor leaves Hispaniola in chains.

Mermaids, dog-headed men and women
with breastplates of copper—
they draw their bows, and arrows

cover the shore of Columbus's dream.
No, not the Taino, whom he once called *in dios*.
They touch his white skin.
They have the faces of Christian angels.

The Door of the Devil

At Puerto del Diablo, the boys
shoot bottles off the cliffs
of pink sandstone and bougainvillea.
In the city, its dusky rose climbs
over the wrought-iron bars that keep out
everything. Fearful of everything,
we push our plates away—the salad
topped with its smear of orange, the man
who pressed his face to our kitchen window.

Morning, and it starts up: the racket
of vendors, the maid's *swish, swish*
as she scrubs out clothes against the stone slab
of the *pila,* mortar fire from the mountains.
I only dream people run through the streets,
past the crazy man with his delicate walk.

The earth shifts beneath the life we wanted:
we work, we work, and turn each night
in to our safe houses. Two by two,
nuns with our downward glances,
we climb and climb, descend
the white streets of the city.

Leaving the Old Gods

I.

The people who watch me hang my coat
on a peg at the office don't even know
about that other life,
the life when there was you, *it,*
however briefly. To them my body
is a fact casual as the weather.
I could tell them:
That day it rained
the way it rains in the New World.
Leaves struck the window like daggers.
I didn't think about *God*
but the ones we used to worship
the ones who want your heart still
beating, who load you with gold
and lure you to sleep
deep in the cenote.

II.

A girl, he said, and I nodded
though we couldn't have known.
I would have left him then
for ten thousand pesos.
I don't know what world you inhabit,
swimming there, baby, not-baby,
part of my body, not me,
swept aside like locks of hair
or toenail parings.
It's ten years today
and you who were never alive
pull a face in the leaves
of the jacaranda, the only tree

that lives outside my window.
It must be your voice
whistling through the office window,
though I can't understand your words.
Comfort or accusation,
I can't understand your words.

The Children's Crusade
El Salvador, The Day of the Dead

The parade begins its black paper circuit.
The humorous dead rise white and fragile
from their shallow boxes. It's bad taste, you tell me,
in a country where everyone's always dying.

You inherit the heyday
of foreign dollars and great houses,
maids who polished your shoes
and wiped your backside until you were twelve.

The parade is moving past us, past the green field
of war where you must not show your face.
Your shadow falls across the pale grass
the soldiers trample.

Tell me again the story of your childhood,
the acres of sweet land, *quinceañeras*
and green mangoes. Tell me even if the words
taste of salt and sting your soft mouth.

The Island of Lost Luggage
Korean Airlines Disaster

for Kevin McNiff

What breeze whispers when you step onto
the black slate of the shore?

And what hooves pound the green valley
beyond the flat beach? *Caribou,* you think,

or *bison in the wild.* A woman in aviator glasses
weaves through the cabanas—a tourist? you wonder

and join the queue from the 747, but you still hear
the roar of the missile, still feel the shock

of cold air. At the head of the line, a clerk
hands you two sets of car keys, a single glove,

an unopened letter mailed so many years ago.
Kevin, some things are lost forever,

and at the Island of Lost Luggage, they line up:
the disappeared, the lost children, the Earharts

of modern life. It's your bad luck to die in the cold
wars of certain nations. But in the line at Unclaimed

Baggage, no one mourns for the sorry world
that sent them here. Memory fails

among these easy trees, beside this sheet of agate
water, where an Ivory Bill calls and calls. . . .

The clerk gestures to a room from your childhood.
Pick up your suitcase and go.

News from the Imaginary Front

Nothing is the latest news of your death.
Shadowed by the five bodies of priests
you disappeared.

You disappeared
quicker than any white person ever
in a country where bodies pile up
so fast they lose count.

We lose count.
50 or 80,000, I can never remember.
But I've seen the photographs.

———————

Reader, you've seen the photographs.
Reader, you've lost count.
90 or 100,000, you can't remember either.

Reader, come closer.
I'll tell the story
the way
I know you want to hear it.

Think this:
It could have been me
Think this:
It could have been any
one of us. It wasn't.

Think chocolate, think coffee.
Reader, it's such a special pleasure—
a return ticket and danger.

Are you pleased about the danger?
Hold tight to your ticket, we're moving
quicker than history.

———————

The truth is: I hardly knew you.
I knew an American face,
a mouth that opened
and spoke English.

———————

Reader, I said hold tight to your ticket.
Don't be afraid but please listen carefully.
For I'm gurneying this story down the long corridor
of your pleasure, past a triage nurse
who says we will survive all this danger.

The story: the year I lived in a tiny, violent country,
a Vietnam for my aimless generation.
Now, I am sadly interesting and beautiful to you.
Now, Reader, you can take my wounds seriously.

———————

a) My students said
   you cried in class.
   They told me
   as I cried, one afternoon,
   sick of the gunfire, sick of . . .
b) heady with the sour red wine
   of Argentina, the click of castanets,
   piñata, toreador, Spanish word *here* ———————
c) I loved those students
   whose parents were murderers.
d) a & b
e) All of the above, except c.
f) *He screamed incessantly. Oh what I've been through!*

———————

Remember this, Reader: Central America was hip
in those years.
We bartered   in the marketplace,
      crept   into $4 hotel rooms
with Europeans   and other strangers.
We softened   the g in Nicaragua.
We learned   to call it   Salvador
without the article.

———————

It's disappearing now, all of it.
The pottery's cracked and bright rebozos
grow dull in the North American sun.

———————

It can't be told, but Reader
I'll tell *you* anyway,
the bombs, the *paros,* the night
Duarte's guards drove us home from the bar.
I shot pool with D'Aubuisson's eldest
who was polite when I beat him.

I'm licking salt from the long wound of history.
This blood is sweet and my mouth's full of it.
I'm milking this body for everything it's worth.

Reader, I'm holding out a pale
North American breast so you can suck too.
I love it when you suck like this,
the sweet milk of death, the salt blood
of someone else's war.

II

The Thousand-Year War

Last of all arose the age of hard iron. . . . Now sailors spread their canvas to the winds, though they had as yet but little knowledge of these, and trees which had once clothed the high mountains were fashioned into ships, and tossed upon the ocean waves, far removed from their own element. The land, which had previously been common to all, like the sunlight and breezes, was now divided up far and wide by boundaries, set by cautious surveyors. . . . All proper affection lay vanquished and, last of the immortals, the maiden Justice left the blood-soaked earth.

—Ovid

I
The Grand Hotel

In those days everything was forbidden.
We traveled anyway, into the heart
of the abandoned countryside to a town
in the mountains, near the lake they now call
Lago Verde. Behind the altar of the dark cathedral,
Simon found the delicate bones of an animal,
crawled in, we imagined, out of the biting
winter wind. At the sound of our voices,
the skeleton collapsed into itself, the way
a house of cards falls when the table is jostled.
Bits of fur rose like fine mist from the animal
we could not identify, and drifted, casual
as the spurs of wild daffodils we blew away
as children, those summers near Anuncio. Sister,
do you remember?
                        In this first Autumn,
I am writing you in a whirl of leaves. Dark violet
and yellow, they fill me with emptiness.
And I am listening for swallows, who call
to each other just now at twilight.

The Grand Hotel overlooked Lago Verde.
Its white and blue sign appeared unchanged,
as if doors might fly open and travelers emerge,
to walk the path around the lake. The bright sun
burned our skin, but it was cold in the stone
hotel. We broke two chairs and built a fire,
warming the room a little.

That room with its impossibly high ceilings!

We talked then of how people once lived
and held each other in the musty bed, beneath two

names carved on the mahogany headboard.
I thought: *I will never forget these names*
and have. How little, Anna, we remember of what
we once knew. We are blessed to forget

unlike Luria's poor patient "S," the man
who remembered everything, and in no particular order.
He swam each day through a thick fog of trivia
and history: the yellow toothbrush his aunt
kept at the summerhouse, formulae for colloidal
suspensions, the weight in grams of the Fabergé egg
lost when they took the Imperial Family to Tsarkoe Seloe.

What I remember is this: Simon brought almonds
and a tin of cocoa from his pack that cool evening.
We had the hard flat bread of travelers and plums
found in the tainted countryside. We ate them anyway.
They say that in March on that mountain, the butterflies
were so thick you could not walk without crushing them.
I keep this image as if it were memory.

In the Grand Hotel, we wandered through hallways,
past photographs askew on their wire hangers,
intricate rosettes carved on the overdoors, floors
of polished, hard green stone. We tried to imagine
the people who built this, then poisoned their fishes.
In that poisoned land, we slept and I tell you
I did no dreaming. Anna, will we remember our past
always? Will we ever walk the dream road
of our childhood, lined with wild rose, the scent
of cape jasmine, to waves iridescent with fishes,
fearful only of the wild cries of ravens?

II
The Bound Children

You, little blank slate,
on which we write our misfortune,
learn the lesson for today:
you are rare enough to be stolen.

Hoarded and tethered
with cord of old dresses,
a hank of cut hair, your lives
pare down to one lean caution:

children lost here are never recovered.
In the careful net of their days,
they invent play and play
at play with forlorn pleasure.

III
Advice to Travelers

All this life you were cold
and shivered down
to the small blue bones
the red marrow heart
of a memory,
the shape of a bat,
it fluttered, caught fire.
Even the cinders burned.

You studied the unworked
flesh of your hands.
Dear Reader:
what are you wishing for
in the lonely city?
City of thieves and sickness,
what are you wishing for?

If it is escape, wait.

When it is late enough,
the moon will rise. Then carry
the lantern in your left hand,
an orange in your right.
The orange is for scent.
Hold the orange to your face.
The lantern is for balance:
never light it. Wait
for the moon. Then:
you will find your way. Then:
you will grow light enough
to vanish.

IV
Paradise

Everything is ours. Everything.
Piles of canned goods without their labels—
green beans or peaches in thick syrup.

We own the moon, God expressionless
as a building, love
and its heavy door of longing.

The children fidget in their sleep.
They dream of what they cannot remember—
a field so green they're frightened.

But I remember hyacinths, flat blue, thick
as a hedge against my aunt's screened-in porch.
The ash, gray and fine as silk,

is drifting like the past we hold onto—
trees shrill with blackbirds, the memory of corn,
of whole bodies of clear blue water.

I don't know whether your body exists
in our landscape, if you were in the yard
planting zinnias or on the threshold

half-turned to unlock the door.
I hope you resemble the quiet posture of sleep.
In the silence we live in

each heart beats too roughly, every breath
is an ocean pushed and pulled by the moon.
In case you wondered

I survived, though I'm always dreaming
of the back of a head, the bus lurching forward.
If I could write you words like *distance*

or *nearby* you would understand everything.
But beyond, the silent earth we inherit
stretches, flat and without motion.

V

Advice to Travelers II

1. When you wake, leave furtively.
   Leave everyone you want to save.

2. Don't look for gratitude
   in the huddled-down white morning light.
   You will stumble and lose your way.

3. Do not dream. Dreams sicken you
   with lies and false memories.

4. Carry a map so worn
   it is open to possibility.

5. Carry a blue flag in your left hand
   since blue is the color of flight.
   Take thread, a sharp needle, pearl buttons
   for the world is in need of mending.

6. Be suspicious of the songs of sparrows
   for there are no sparrows.

VI
The Travelers

I.

How did we come here?

We fled. Not the way animals flee from sudden noises or field charged with fire.

But laughing: Schoolchildren during tornado drills. Federal employees after a bomb scare.

We laughed until the mud sucked our heels so hard we could only walk slowly. Then we left things.

In the mud: tea kettles, irons, a bicycle helmet.

Finally: shoes, jewelry, photographs.

II.

Flimsy as the reeds that scratch her bony cheekbone, the world is a hank of hair, bluestem rising between stalks of white straw, not dead, rising. When we knew we were dying, the world pared down to an essential landscape. Our hearts grew light when the burden of trying to save ourselves lifted.

III.

A man and a woman enter that landscape, moving clumsily beneath their winter clothes. Their shadows are blue on the white ice.

This story is our thick skin of sorrow.

At the edge of their journey, a swing swings empty and the wind is sharp and no one calls or answers. All night branches rake the sky and trees creak against the cold, surge and burnish the white air. They breathe the tainted air of yesterday, the chill wind of tomorrow.

This journey. The way back. The gate back to childhood. She whispers: *Brother, we will find it.*

VII
Seven

I. COMMUNION

Take this bowl of memory between your hands.

Sweet milk and strawberries in the garden of childhood,
the round bowl we are passing
keeps Death away,
outside the circle of our circle.

II. PLAGUE

Death sweeps the country clean of untainted life.
In the landscape of bodies, boils turn inward.
Blackened skin is crosshatched with desperate scratching.
Pilgrims cast out all the wrong devils.
They marry false angels.

III. CRUSADE

She writes: Come home to the dying. Come home
before everyone you ever loved
dies of it.

At the inn, they hold white kerchiefs
against the smell, burn incense to scrub clean
a world made sick with evil.

IV. FEAST

How cold it is in the world beyond memory.

How silent, beyond the stone walls,
after the storm has stopped.
Guests, make ready,
for the table is laid.
Bring all your best hungers
and we will pick this animal to the bone,

wash it down with red, full-bodied wine,
lick our fingers over the greasy carcass.

V. A GAME OF CHESS

Death will not answer your questions, sweet Traveler.
The game is luck, chance, skill, and luck.
Why play? When the storm rises,
the board will buckle, the pieces scatter
black and white.

VI. WITCH-BURNING

Advice to travelers:
Avoid the South for there is pestilence.
Avoid the North for they will burn you for a witch.

One angel has a beautiful skull, taut against
her freshly shaved scalp. It melts to nothing
in the hot fire of the witch-burning.
A man takes pity and pushes his sword
between her ribs, through her fluttering heart.

All of the angels cry from their cages.
But if they are innocent, God is guilty.

VII. SEVEN

An hourglass, a sundial, a scythe, a silver bracelet. Milk, strawberries,
    incense.

Tell the survivors the story of perishing.
Tell the next world of plague, war, hunger, death, God, good, and evil.

The survivors are shadows in the west,
where there is no sky, only horizon.

VIII

The Thousand-Year War

Imagine, if you will, a people sleeping.
Imagine how, when the weather changed,
we shrugged
and went about our leisure.
Then: earth, sky, water.
Everything
changed color.
We looked away, uneasy.

When next we looked, we saw the fields
grow dry and empty,
that long September into Autumn,
the Winter Years that followed.
We grow small: a people who die
faster than they are born.

We say that no one lives beyond the border,
the line that separates
where one may never live
from here, where one may live a little.
The few who left have not returned.

I am writing you this letter,
though you may never write to me.
From grief or sorrow, I doubt
I'll ever know. I try to remember you,
in a time that cannot bear remembering.
But this I know: the sunsets
grew more beautiful, not less, the rain
was gradual and warm. Fat, fat
was our final Autumn.
The fruit was rich and orange.

Now things wear down. The things
we used to love wear down.
Bit by bit, we push the clutter
beyond the fenced-in territory.
There you might find anything:
clever metal gadgets
whose use has been forgotten,
a vase of peacock feathers,
books of pictures
no one has the will to open.

Imagine a world pared down to Winter.
Imagine, if you can, a land
that sighed, turned over,
and slept another thousand years.
In the time left us,
will we speak?
Will we ever speak of it?

III

A Map of the Twentieth Century

Even the small trees you planted as children
have long since become too heavy; you could not
carry them now. But the winds . . . But the spaces. . . .
—RILKE

The Monster of Childhood

In the house of your childhood, the blue monster
leaned over the iron railing and the red one hid,
the way monsters hide, in the space beneath the bed.
All night they gobbled the air you tried to breathe.
They shed dust bunnies, they groaned, their nails
grew long and yellow, as they tapped out
camp songs, lullabies—all night they tapped:
Make New Friends, The Farmer in the Dell.

I am not the mother, the father, the sister in this story.
I am not: Djinn, Mage, Fairy Godmother, Sorcerer.
Only the monsters are real in this story. They sweat

blue and red over the boy in the narrow bed.
I would chase the blue one with an owl feather duster.
I would tell the red one, Off With You!
there are other boys to bother.

But let's call this memoir, and say in this memoir,
and say, if you listen, a door is
creaking open. There's the sound of glass breaking,
a wooden soldier drumming, a stuffed bear's
thud and tumble. Vines climb the wall
that leads to your window, but there is no escape
through the wooden wardrobe, no secret
world below, no key, no underground tunnel.

The wind outside is a real wind, not pretend.
In it, the trees of childhood make a terrible sound.

The Children's Corner

The game is pretend. The dark cape of Superman
flares as you run. It snaps in the January wind.
We are tired superheroes, picking our way
among the cow patties in Grandmother's pasture.
When you were six, you took your third tumble,
this time face first, through a basement window,
but carry only a thin scar on your cheekbone
and a furrow beneath your chin.
                              In the failing light
we turn toward home for supper and *The Children's Corner*.
The record starts with "Stone Soup," a tale of a stone
boiled to feed three soldiers and a hungry village.

We know about selfishness, but not greed,
know about hunger, but not starvation. We know
about fear—the monster on the airplane wing,
white face pressed to the glass. Now you tell planes
when to land, and they come down gracefully,
intact, and free of gremlins.
                              Tonight, the game is flight
and sweat beads the palms of my hands during takeoff.

Fear is not so simple now, enough could ground
a plane forever. Who would fly, anyway? Not me,
I think, turning my face once more toward the aisle,
wondering if I show up on your radar screen,
wondering if *it*'s out there, wrenching up sheet
after sheet of metal, willing this plane to the ground.
Captain Kirk cannot save himself, and the story
spins out, black and white, the Sixties TV monster
quaint in his fur costume.
                              We are still the same children,
unchanged, despite hospitals and jail, despite spouses

who hurt us. You're always just out of sight.
I saw you a month ago at a concert and I stumbled
coke-weary, face burning across the amphitheater,
but you were gone. You'd never offer me a joint anymore,
but take your drugs from prescription bottles,
so much oil on the waters of a troubled marriage.

We had a dozen safe years and enter, each morning,
a world grown still with longing. Turn back, brother,
I want to call after you, turn back.
It's a desperate journey you choose to call love.
I can't call it love but then I turn from everything,
starved by a happy childhood, our sad legacy.

The Lean Year

In the west room of an old house
we are sorting out china.
I have been washing all morning,
an old story and for you
not a good one.
It's a different life you remember:
men are peeling shrimp
when you walk out to the end
of the pier.

For a year I've dreamed of houses.
Your hands look foreign tonight.
We are watching a bird
fly across the river, when you turn to me
and say, this year, home doesn't
keep very well. Friend,
there's something wrong with October.
We both know it, but today,
it is what you will not say.
Last night while it was still
I drove my car down into the mire.
Somewhere it is autumn and leaves
are falling thick as bees.

It is dark outside. I am walking
toward home. Your heart is a clock
that doesn't tick very well.
You've handed me back to the past.
This autumn, even the birds
have stayed home, and the seed
they did not find slips into the dirt
of a lean year. There are days
when we can forget all but this color,

this leaf, or the appearance
of small stones under water.
It is not enough.
I think your life will always matter.

Birthday

for my brother

The jobs you cannot or will not keep
come back with small voices from the house
of our parents. This summer, success

means so much; like a doll's dress, a lost
letter, so much comes out of the past.
By the light from my window, we can see

that it is getting late. Miles from here
a woman in a dark room slips off
her pearl earrings. Her hands are lined

with veins, but it is my birthday.
This morning, as you cook me breakfast
your eyes are someone else's. Nights

I'm afraid. David, the windows are dirty.
You clear the house of bats and remind me
that I will always be younger than you.

The Venus Thread

Here is the gold coin spinning.
It gains dimension, fills out, a world
metallic and full of light. Yellow,
the egg explodes, the monthly
half-day agony, goodbye she waves
to each possibility, the globe stuffed full,
blood clotting in the endless
hot bath.

The coin has rough edges. It isn't gold.
But a Mardi Gras doubloon, dull nickel
under the patina of gilt
which flakes off in the boy's pocket
carried clear to Sweet Thursday
along the waterfront where the rats grow big
as loaves of bread.

   • • •

pinch me in case I might be
dreaming   hurt my body *here*
so my pain will have a way to listen
the birches are white in the twilight
the naked bodies of white people watching
the white bodies of naked people
not watching, but listening
the green curtains rustle

   • • •

She who is left holding hearts
or the Queen of Spades loses.
Hearts once were Cups, a hundred years
before you were born, little dealer.

The suit that could be filled or emptied,
inverted in the 7, but the Ace—

ah, there everything emerges,
rainbow, flower, a hand pointing skyward.

    • • •

After your family left town
we played in the empty house, my brother and I.
We crept into the bedroom that had been yours.
He found the web of a used-up nylon
in your mother's bedroom closet
and a pink plastic comb
wound with your blond hair.

    • • •

The venus thread will cut
the circulation, left too long
on a ring finger, a blue reminder.
Spun, stretched out, thin and fine,
bitten off by sharp white teeth,
not yours, but someone's.

    • • •

I'm on a train riding backwards.
This way the world recedes.
Objects disappear just as
they enter your field of vision.
The woman across from me leans into the window
face forward into every small town we pass.
We never linger.
Stranger, we have three games in common:
Scissors, Rock & Paper, I am counting my fist
three times into my palm, hoping you will notice

as the fingers flatten out, ready to cover or be cut.
I know Red Rover, the game we never played
once my cousin broke her wrist.
Tic Tac Toe, the game you cannot lose.

Stranger, if they send someone over,
will our hands hold fast or will we break apart
ready to welcome them, to change
who we are, what we will become?

A Child's Geography

After we had language you
never touched us and the years spun away
fast. One child was nearly thirty
before you looked up
as a shadow passed
across the pages of your open book.
There's a dream I'd remind you of
from that week you were more dead than alive.
We washed your dry mouth
with a cloth soaked in cool water.
In your dream the ocean
sectioned out like an orange
the ribs of an umbrella
opening and closing. You opened your eyes,
but you were still in that dream, weren't you?
In the ICU lounge, some daughters
camp out for days. When we knew you'd live,
I descended the twelve floors of the hospital,
and between the sleeping bags and pink curlers,
saw their earnest faces wound tight
in a dream. My mother said:
Kiss your father before you go.
When I do, our flesh is light,
unanchored by the past, the green field
of memory where we float and cannot find
a place to land.

A Map of the Twentieth Century

I. FATHER

Tomorrow's the twentieth century. Your brothers
nail the last board of the new schoolhouse.
One twin leans into the wall, fills his lungs
with the smell of pine, which stings
on this cool and out of season morning.
Your father smells snow in the gray clouds
though it never snows here for Christmas.
He waves as he heads back down the mountain
to bring back the teacher, a girl
to teach his boys to read and write,
what Tom Martin, with his forceful X,
never learned.

II. GRANDFATHER

Your sister leaves the room whispering *Not true,*
not true, at the thought of Indian skin
against the white skin of her grandmother.
Three generations later we are pale as sand.
Third Thursdays we hover at the banquet table
filling our bodies with yams and sweet corn.
We dream him up
                       from yellowed records
that crumble at a touch, twelve thousand names
that Jackson drove to Oklahoma. They dropped
like flies swatted in the heat of summer.
But it was cold, and when they dropped,
they dropped to snow. He stayed and took
the one name *Moses,* that most conjures up
the laws by which they could not live.

III. NURSE

This room is cold as death. This room is death,
cold as a year in the Argonne Forest.

43

I'm freezing, you whisper, freezing to death.
The nurse's palm is cool against your forehead.
At her touch, the room comes into focus:
four middle-aged daughters argue
at the room's only window,
which speaks of hot summer, not winter.
In the Argonne Forest, it is always winter,
waiting for replacements, waiting
for the chance to live again.

IV. BATTLEFIELD

No, it's impossible to imagine, the distance between France and Cleburne County, Alabama. But how do you know you're here, how do you know where you are, when the world is small as a map or else as large as days and days. The place where you know everyone. Where you come in from the cold to a woodstove burning hickory. No, it's impossible to imagine in all this death and biting cold. The Argonne Forest. Now you are the Argonne Forest, you are the left leg of your partner, twenty yards from his body, which lies stiff and unbreathing. Or the black horse looming over the edge of the trench. No, not a horse, a tree, broken in the shelling, broken over and over from the looks of it. I will never get these boots off, my feet will never be warm, maybe they are waiting for me in the trenches up ahead, or maybe everyone is dead, maybe everyone is dead.

V. DESCENDENTS

The last time we checked, one Thanksgiving,
eighty years after your war,
there were thirty descendents, fifteen of us
grandchildren. When we travel,
we take luggage and drink margaritas
on beaches that resemble pictures of beaches.

We don't know the story of the Argonne Forest.
We make up the snow, the boy who died.
We make up the plane you jumped from.

In the hunter's camp,
on the land we took and claim,
and take back and claim again,
we dream all the lost bodies of happiness and sorrow—
flesh, bone, and sinew of a dozen generations—
you had one brown grandfather and one
who kept his white robes
hidden beneath the iron bedstead.
Some of the dead are too useful for sympathy.
The past we own exists on stone and white paper.

IV

After the War

The moon is my mother. She is not sweet like Mary.

—Sylvia Plath

A Woman Speaks to Her Past

Lies make us up like a bed no one's slept in.
I dreamed we walked a city street
past alleys of rubbish. You refused
to hold my hand and over us
the sky flapped the color of bleached sheets.

Here, a mural peels off the face of a building,
half brick, half a story we don't
begin to understand. The crowded street
is empty for once, quiet as if everything
had just moved out of sight.

You've never particularly wanted to be anything.
This alley is heavy with smoke and clouds
the air between us and the path we trace back.
I write this letter to tell you everything,
but it is you who must speak.

The Book of Days and Nights

FIRST NIGHT

The World beyond the page is yellow, the day is blue.
Trees hum a tune of sorrow and the father
opens his heavenly body. Skin parts
beneath the surgeon's knife, shines like
the stilled pond, the silver plate, a face
gazing back in shadow. Caught in the silver frame, I, I, I,
who will soon walk away from myself.

MONDAY: FALSE OF HEART, LIGHT OF EAR

Lines we cast, dust that stings our eyes, hooks in
the greasy red heart of our desire.
What about bells?
What about the whistle that says

    Come here now
    Behave yourself
    Walk slowly
    Stop
    Stop right where you are.

SECOND DAY

A bird whistles. You could not call that singing.
I have seen hawks flying
backpedaling
when the wind is gusty. But birds here
are tiny and seldom seen. They cry
from their delicate cages, vermillion
and yellow green, in the dirty marketplace.

A LITTLE FIRE, A WILD FIELD

When I was a child, we could often see
lights moving down the mountain

like fireflies, lonely yellow
against the dark blue night.

Like light diffused through air
as thick as water.

NEXT DAY
Stale, the hard loaf of our day
left in the sun too long. A melon
cleaved open, the blood-red heart of things.
Death is a torn curtain, a frayed cloth
for washing. Do you remember
the days when stone could talk?

FRIDAY: POOR TOM THAT EATS THE SWIMMING FROG
Boy children are all around you.
They reach through the barred windows.
They grab at you, you grab, you pull
the smallest one through

and shake him, roughly.
First by the back of his neck,
then by his small tough foot.
He shakes like a doll.
He is younger than the youngest child you know.

SATURDAY
My heart grows scales
and swims like a fish through my body.

I think:
I may be sleeping.

The first war I ever fought
was in a bedroom, the enemy
a man I loved, who slapped and hit

and held me down
and held me down.

Listen:
I am sleeping, I am dreaming.
I am dreaming
someone else's dream.

OCEAN, AFTERNOON
Sleep now in the parched sea of childhood.
That gate we can open, we can.

Past the stiff air of wakening
to where the color blue is beckoning.
They say the mermaids left the lake. They live
like tiny brides on first communion day.

This is not metaphor.
Not:
leather, velvet, dull gray iron
but skin with no love of breaking.

Hunger

What could I say to you that day
I knew I was leaving? The Chicago shore sweeps into
the lake's blue plummet, and water drifts in
sure as your certain gaze. After our uneasy evenings,
that night across the restaurant table—
I couldn't touch my food—

I know how much and in what ways
you might hurt me. I choked on my hot soup,
pushed the Pol Tak around on my plate
while three tourists hovered in the doorway
guessing the characters on the restaurant's
red banner. *Good luck!* I wanted to shout.
It always means good luck, another way of saying
May you never look back.
You pushed the food toward me

but what do you know about hunger?
People die and walk around. The plane hums on the runway.
You have your urgent story. When I rise,
you are dreaming, intent on the first spuft
of fire from your cigarette.
After the terror of take off, I settle into my seat
as the plane banks the white clouds over Lake Michigan.

After the War

I. DROWNING
I loved you in ways you
cannot begin to imagine. Only that once
a flash of tension behind your calm eyes,
the kind of tension that grips my stomach
before the last wave flattens me
and drags me toward shore. I struggle

and remember you pushing my face under,
long hair streaming, wrapping your wrist,
a memory for today, when I write from a place
made safe by time and distance.
I wish I had let you kill me.

II. THE LATE SHOW
Memory crawls from every muscle in my body.
I wake with a fist in my stomach
as the sky rows down
the difficult hours toward dawn.

The day we left each other, the sky
was a bright, bright blue, the day heady
with relief. I walked down the narrow street,
heels laconic on the flat gray of the sidewalk.

You drifted around a corner,
thinking about anything, I imagined,
your '64 Buick, the year the Grateful Dead
played Memphis, a sharkskin suit you bought
from a guy in the jungle and lost
on the plane coming home.

III. THE POLITICS OF COMPASSION
My youth and your hard destiny.
The year they closed the Boaz Double View,

your girlfriend and half the senior class
got pregnant. I was fourteen then,
stumbling around a different town
in a haze of drugs and bad intentions.
I've seen the letter you sent her,
the day after you flew out over
the unbelievable green of Vietnam.
In our time together, you crawled
from one bottle to another,
slapped my face until it stung.
This is what it's like now—I turn, each night,
to a safe bed with a man my own age.
I find so little anger finally,
only the hard green stone of compassion,
medicine taken again and again.

IV. FUNERAL RITES

My fingers are like sticks and I don't mind
the way these women touch my body,
drape flimsy silk across my hips, rub oil

into my skin until it shines . . . my fingers
are like sticks, and when I hold them out
across the stack of balsa, smoke rises between them

like thin gray scarves. In the distance,
the flat boats of fishermen are moving along the pier,
and the fire roars in my ears, like the ocean

after all, like the roar of the helicopter
moving the green tops of trees. How long it took
that year I was with you, that year I burned.

Heart

I found your letter after a long month
traveling. When I step into the bath,
I take the one page with me, push it under,
watch the blue letters, the old word *love,*
rise toward me like so much smoke.

Tonight, when we put our bodies together,
it is like any night. You unlace
the sad cotton of my dress, pull me
into the unmade bed. I suck your neck so hard
a piece of flesh comes off in my mouth. My earring
catches in your beard, tears clean through the lobe.
I am happy enough to lie here after, palms down,
spine flat against the hard bed, each gust of wind
flinging the sheer curtains over our bodies.

The cedars stir, dusting the windowsill
with new snow. The red jacket of the neighbor's son
is moving through the trees in the far part
of the yard. He fires his air gun
and startles the last pair of Lord Gods.

The heart is lonely
and thumps in its separate cage,
cage we call body. My heart is lean and can run
for miles without my body, but your heart
runs on hunger, a solid muscle
over its four empty, fragile chambers.

A Disturbance in Memory

*You have to begin to lose your memory, to realize that without it, we
are nothing. . . . I can only wait for the final amnesia, the one that
can erase an entire life.—Luis Buñuel*

I. THE PATH TO THE MEADOW
   AUGUST 1914
We walk through the shadow,
through the cool air. Pine trees
dip their heavy branches
down to me. I have
a basket with a green cloth,
wine and food enough.

You've brought me here twice,
my skirt catching on brambles,
along the uneven path
to the meadow. You push,
push me back into the grass.
We will not come here again.

II. CONFESSION
    AUGUST 1926
Listen, Doctor, I tell you
he was nothing, my husband.
He was nothing to me.
Here are his letters—

that long year in Fairhope,
those months I waited . . .
it came down to the one night
I refused to undress
and he pushed his body into me
anyway. He was nothing
yet days I wish I had the listless

foreign eyes that might have
held him here.

III. THE CHILD'S BODY

DREAM, SEPTEMBER 1914
You said look, but I would not look.

When I looked, the child's body
floated by us again and again.
We were sitting on the rooftop,
yellow mud rising, staining
the hem of my dress.

You said:

> *the wrist is thin and bone*
> > *wrap it with silk*
> *and it is flesh*
> > *you no longer have to own*

IV. AIR

AUGUST 1926
There were the heirlooms
to consider,
the child we did not have.
There was no money, no money,
no air, no arm to take.

Doctor, after he left me alone
he left me *alone*. I heard
a faint whisper when I stepped
from the train in Vienna.

V. THREE DRESSES

DREAM, NOVEMBER 1914
In the closet, there are three
long dresses: the stiff blue taffeta
for parties, the yellow pinafore
for breakfast by the pond.

The white dress, worn once,
rustles in its muslin bag.

VI. DANCES

   DREAM, FEBRUARY 1927
She ties the corsage to her wrist,
pulls tight the white string
of her lace glove. Faint music

stirs the petals of wisteria
that hangs from the balustrade
and soldiers line up

the color of dust in this heat.
She was tired of the heat,
of the vague colors of August.

VII. THE STORY OF MARRIAGE

   JANUARY 1915
If you marry me, though it's you
who ask, it will be grudgingly.
A ring with a clear stone, stone

you gaze through to the finger
of one who has never liked diamonds.
I think of white organza,

dresses lined up like so many
rasping stalks of wheat.
When we marry

you will begrudge me everything.
I am a woman.
It is not a matter of choice.

VIII. MERMAID

   DREAM, JUNE 1927
We followed her
her white lace dress

a cloud
among all the brambles.
It was so hot
and once I thought
I saw a scarred, bony ankle
flash below the hem.
You said *Hurry*
but we are too late.
She vanishes into the sea
and she is fish
from the knees down,
her fins a scratch
across my forehead.

IX. MEMORY

JUNE 1927

If he had been good to me
that summer, I'm sure the sky
would not now refuse to close in

rolling like soot across the rooftops
of these thin summer houses.
Nor would the willows dip

and dip at me. They drink
the green water without permission.
Doctor, a basket left there one summer

is cracked with age and bad weather.
I'd like to pull at my wrist
'til the one bad hand

dangled by a thread.
And then I would be free,
free and light as air.

X. THE UNDATED DREAM

I am drifting down from a blue, blue sky—
a piece of white ash on a still wind,
the sun blazing off the sea
moving so gradually to meet me.
The sea swims with mercy and weakness.
Doctor, what does it mean
to land finally,
to land in a dream?
I am falling into the most
unimaginable blue
and nothing will rouse me
from such calm water.

Cemetery Autumn
"There is no winter here of heart."

PRELUDE: THREE WIVES' SONNET
The wives did not survive. Over their graves
one of the two rosemary bushes
grew green and thick, but the other
dropped from its marble pedestal. Tourists
breathe the fragrant air as they arrive
to photograph the beautiful, irregular plot.
But the wives did not survive.

Ella, Kizziah, Nettie Redwine—they lie
like railroad cars across the way
from Mr. Blake. In safe stone crypts
they lie, worn out or dead
by childbirth. In bitter, east Texas winters,
those children did not thrive.
But the wives did not survive.

I.
This September, lovebugs over east Texas
flock Oak Grove's marble tombs.
Among the elm and cedar,
a woman carries a wreath for her quarter-acre past,
for men who took and held and fenced the land.
The Caddo linger in a single mound

in wooden effigy passed hand to hand
by drunken boys at football games.
Large as grapefruit, hard as stone,
bois d'arc balls stack the space
between one wife's feet
and another's reddish hair.

II.

Even this late in the evening, Nettie's crypt
is warm against the bones and muscles
of my back. The Pleiades catch
in the branches of a century-old oak
I once counted the steps around.

The youngest bride of all,
if Nettie died in childbirth,
there is no sleeping lamb,
no small stone here to mark the story.

III.

That autumn, twilight at the Blake graves
was my heart's worst loneliness.

That endless fall, you and the dead
were my only companions.

Those afternoons, birds called only to each other.
The one white angel looked away.

IV.

A century-old tree dwarfs
mausoleum, angel, crypt,
its girth too wide for us
to join our hands on either side of it.

This tree, this metaphor
for everything not right between us.
This tree that shades a corner of east Texas,
the place we are so out of place
we think we are together.

Not you, I thought
while the warm stone scratched my back.

While a man I wanted to love
slept a thousand miles away
in the shadow of a skyscraper.

Dry your eyes, I told myself, it is pollen
not sorrow.
Rise and go: it is not fatigue
but September's dead heat.
It is not love,
but heat only heat.

Flood

We drive the car into the next morning,
over a distance we're happy
to lose sight of. Memory rises with the river,
and brown water fills the fields,
turned to stubble in the cold.
The arc of the bridge is too high to look back.
The river rises and drives us, the forced sing-along,
your foot heavy on the gas pedal.
There were no stars last night. I pass time
rummaging through what we chose to take:
this story, a few battered pots and pans,
one lamp—its aqua shade turned up.

Everything will disappear into this thick water,
into last night when we told each other
what we had kept secret for years.
It's dangerous to dream along, to ignore
natural disaster. We point the car
toward the horizon, wanting to be a point
on its line, a place of motion, nothing more.

The Signs of Leaving

I. COUNTING ARMADILLOS

Beside the highway, vultures pick them down
to delicate, hematite shells.
A helmet emptied of its flesh,
one rocks like a cradle
just past Carthage
as the semis fly by.

II. MOVES

The mover wants to sleep with me.
Ours is the best kind of marriage:
room by room we pack this house,
the things I bought, took, was given
for the life I planned to start here.
We take turns bringing back coffee
and plain cake donuts from the Krispy Kreme
until I drive away behind his yellow van,
past medians choked with oxalis.

III. THE CHANGE STONE

Weren't there two cities?
The one where I strolled
hands in pockets,
red brick streets
all night all night?

The whispered sleepless city
and the one I entered, each day,
into the blazing sunlight?

In the square, the fingers of slaves
mark a row of bricks. Names etch
the newer ones: a local businessman,
the Baptist church, Mrs. Wilson's

fifth-grade class, who collected pennies
and sold stale chocolate door to door.

IV. THE BLACK SILK JACKET

In the stiff photograph, six bone buttons
lie dull against the woman's jacket,
so perfect it ages everything around it:
the woman, her twin sisters, the rose settee
where they pose for an unknown photographer.

What could it be, the scrap of paper in her hand?
A recipe for spice cake—the one they served
at Christmas and family weddings? The lien
never paid? A note to the elements saying:
Sun, this year let the corn grow and grow or
Wind, sweep down the empty plain
and take it all: there is nothing for us here.

V. LEAVING

I leave the photograph in the left-hand pocket
of the black silk jacket. I leave
the woman with my face
and close the empty house and drive away.
High in my neighbor's oak, two young barred owls
turn their furious faces from me.

And drive past men in jeans and cowboy hats
who jingle keys in their pockets,
past the rosemary bushes lining the cemetery
thick with the graves of women who stayed.
Only these things, nothing more.
On I-35, I roll down the window
and open my hand to the wind.
I let them go. I let them all go.

Notes

"The Basilica of Our Lady of Good Health" is set in Pátzcuaro, Mexico. Gertrudis Bocanegra was a young woman martyred in the Mexican Revolution, and one of Pátzcuaro's two plazas is named for her. The tree to which she was bound when she faced the Spanish firing squad is still standing and can be found in the central plaza.

"Boulevard of Heroes," "The Door of the Devil," and "News from the Imaginary Front" refer to events that took place in El Salvador during the late 1980s, when José Napoleon Duarte was president. "Boulevard of Heroes" truncates into a single weekend a number of events that took place in 1987 and 1988 in response to the Esquipulas II Peace Talks, including the *paros* (from the Spanish verb *parar* "to stop"), by which the leftist FMLN closed down the capital, and the assassination of the head of the Salvadoran human rights agency by the right. El Puerto del Diablo ("door of the Devil") is a peak just outside the capital city of San Salvador that affords a stunning view of the surrounding countryside. During the early 1980s, it was notorious as a dumping ground for bodies of the disappeared. The guerillas of the left-wing FMLN were often referred to as "the boys." Founder of the right-wing ARENA Party, Roberto D'Aubuisson has, according to Amnesty International, "been accused of active participation in the activities of the death squads responsible for the death of thousands of Salvadoreans, including the assassination of Archbishop Oscar Romero."

"The Hands of the Taino" concerns the punishment Christopher

Columbus doled out to Indians who could not meet their annual gold quota, during his tenure as governor of Hispaniola.

The title "The Island of Lost Luggage" is taken from an episode of *Saturday Night Live*. Unlike that episode, the poem is about the shooting down of Korean Airlines flight 007 by the Soviets. Evidence eventually emerged to suggest that KAL 007, at the request of U.S. intelligence agencies, deliberately strayed into Soviet air space to test Soviet defensive radar systems. In the poem, reference is made to several endangered or extinct animals, among them the great ivory-billed woodpecker.

PART II. THE THOUSAND-YEAR WAR

"The Thousand-Year War" is a sequence of poems set in a post–environmental holocaust landscape. A. R. Luria, who is mentioned in "The Grand Hotel," was a Russian psychologist whose fascinating *The Mind of a Mnemonist* recounts the case study of "S," the man who could forget nothing. I am grateful to Norman Ellis for bringing Luria's work to my attention.

The poem "Seven" is based loosely on Ingmar Bergman's film *The Seventh Seal*.

PART III. A MAP OF THE TWENTIETH CENTURY

"The Children's Corner" focuses on a particular episode of *The Twilight Zone:* "Terror at 20,000 Feet." In that episode, the lead is played by William Shatner, who later became famous as Captain Kirk of the starship *Enterprise*.

PART IV. AFTER THE WAR

While "A Disturbance in Memory" is the name of an actual case study by Freud, this poem relates an entirely different narrative.

"Lord God" (from the poem "Heart") is the name by which the pileated woodpecker is known in the South.

The area of east Texas described in "Cemetery Autumn" was originally Caddo Indian land. There is now a single small burial mound in someone's front yard; the other mounds were excavated, and their contents are housed on the campus of Stephen F. Austin State University in Nacogdoches, Texas. Students at the school have a life-sized wooden Indian nicknamed "Chief Caddo," which is passed to the winning team of the annual SFASU–Southeastern Louisiana football game. Efforts by the Native American student organization at SFASU to stop this practice have been futile.

Acknowledgments

My thanks to the editors of the following magazines and anthologies, where some of these poems first appeared, sometimes in different versions:

Ascent: "The Monster of Childhood"

Asylum: "Heart"

Birmingham Poetry Review: "A Woman Speaks to Her Past"

Bottomfish: "The Children's Crusade" and "The Hands of the Taino"

Chili Verde: "Birthday" and "Hunger"

Columbia: "The Grand Hotel"

Flint Hills Review: "The Lean Year"

Folio: "The Signs of Leaving"

High Plains Literary Review: "Boulevard of Heroes" (under the title "Manifestations")

The Indiana Review: "Paradise"

Many Mountains Moving: "News from the Imaginary Front"

Mobius: "The Thousand-Year War"

Negative Capability: "A Disturbance in Memory"

North American Review: "The Children's Corner"

Outsiders: Poems about Rebels, Renegades, and Exiles (Milkweed Press): "Leaving the Old Gods"

Poetry: "Flood"

Sundog: "Cemetery Autumn"

TriQuarterly: "After the War," "Leaving the Old Gods," and "El Salvador del Mundo"

Webster Review: "A Child's Geography"

The Women's Review of Books: "The Basilica of Our Lady of Good Health"

Grateful acknowledgment is made to the Alabama State Council for the Arts for a Writer's Fellowship and to the Georgia Council for the Arts for an Individual Artist's Fellowship. I would also like to thank Norcroft, the MacDowell Colony, the Ragdale Foundation, and the Virginia Center for the Creative Arts. I am grateful to the University of Oklahoma and Stephen F. Austin State University for grants to travel to these colonies.

I would like to thank Ellen Arnold, Pamela Barnett, Nicole Cooley, Lynn Domina, Ben Ellis, David Ellis, Emily Ellis, Kay Ellis, Norman Ellis, Patricia Penn Hilden, Geary Hobson, Julie Kubala, David Lowe, Eric Moe, and Susan Thomas.

Bob Taylor

JANET MCADAMS's poems have appeared in *Poetry, TriQuarterly,* the *North American Review, Many Mountains Moving, Nimrod, Columbia,* the *Women's Review of Books,* the *Atlanta Review, Ascent,* the *Crab Orchard Review,* and the anthology *Outsiders: Poems about Rebels, Renegades, and Exiles* (Milkweed Press). Her poetry has earned her fellowships from both the Alabama and the Georgia state arts councils, and she has been a resident at the MacDowell Colony, Norcroft, Ragdale, and the Virginia Center for the Creative Arts. She received a Ph.D. in comparative literature from Emory University and an M.F.A. in creative writing from the University of Alabama. Of mixed Scottish, Irish, and Creek ancestry, she grew up in Alabama and presently teaches Native American literature and creative writing at the University of Oklahoma.